the **complete** *series*

Vegetarian

WILEY

John Wiley & Sons, Inc.

For general information on our other products and services or for technical support, please contact our Customer Care Department within the United States at (800) 762-2974, outside the United States at (317) 572-3993 or fax (317) 572-4002.

Wiley also publishes its books in a variety of electronic formats. Some content that appears in print may not be available in electronic books. For more information about Wiley products, visit our web site at www.wiley.com.

Library of Congress Cataloging-in-Publication Data is available upon request.

ISBN 978-1-118-11978-5

Printed in China

10 9 8 7 6 5 4 3 2 1

Contents

Introduction

Vegetarian eating is a healthy alternative for today's lifestyle. Whether you are a strict vegetarian or a meat eater striving for a more health-conscious, planet-friendly way to eat, this book is for you. Meals without meat, poultry or seafood are tasty, satisfying, and best of all—good for you. The delectable dishes in this book are hearty enough to stand on their own. You'll never miss the meat!

Vegetable know-how

To make the most of your garden-fresh vegetables, we have put together essential step-by-step preparation and cooking tips to help you create delicious veggie dishes.

Ready

Easy cooking and preparation depends on having a few good basic pieces of equipment. To make life easier for you it is worth investing a little time and money in some good equipment such as a large chopping board, a small sharp vegetable or paring knife, several larger sharp knives for cutting and chopping, a grater; a vegetable peeler and a colander or large sieve. Remember to keep your knives sharp – either learn to sharpen them yourself or take them to a knife sharpener regularly. Sharp knives make preparation a breeze.

Set

Wash vegetables before preparing, but do not soak. Soaking tends to draw out the valuable water-soluble vitamins and you end up with vegetables with a lower nutrient content. As with most rules there are always exceptions and it may be necessary to soak very dirty vegetables to remove dirt and creepie crawlies. If this is the case, always keep soaking times to a minimum.

- Vegetables that are left whole with their skins on have a higher nutrient and fiber content than those that are finely chopped and peeled. Many of the precious vitamins and minerals found in vegetables are stored just under the skin. Only peel vegetables if necessary.

- For maximum nutritional value, prepare vegetables just before cooking and serve as soon as they are cooked.

- The smaller the portion, the quicker the cooking time. For example, grated carrot will cook more quickly than carrot cut into slices.

Go

Here's how:

- To cube, cut into about ½ inch/1cm pieces.
- To dice, cut into ¼ inch/0.5cm pieces.
- To mince, cut into ⅛ inch/0.25cm pieces.
- To grate, use either a hand grater or a food processor with a grating attachment.
- To slice, cut very thin or thick. You can also slice into rings. Another way to slice is to cut diagonally. This is a good way to prepare vegetables such as carrots, celery and zucchini for stir-frying.

Remember the three Ms

- Minimum water
- Minimum cooking
- Minimum cutting

Good for you

Health authorities recommend that we eat four servings of vegetables daily, at least one of which should be raw. The old adage of a white, a yellow and a green may be rarely taught these days, but it is a good reminder that the brightly colored vegetables are usually the best source of vitamins.

Pantry planning

Try the following tips for no-fuss pantry planning.

- If you store herbs and spices in alphabetical order, they are easily located and you can quickly see when they need replacing.
- Growing a few herbs of your own such as basil, cilantro, rosemary, mint, chives and parsley means that you always have these on hand. These fresh herbs are often the secret to bright, delicate flavors in meals.
- Place all staples, such as sugar and flour, together. Groups sauces and condiments according to cuisines so you'll be inspired when you look at them.
- Keep a good selection of frozen vegetables. Peas, beans, spinach and corn are great standbys and only take minutes to cook in the microwave.
- Keep a variety of breads and rolls in the freezer and defrost in the microwave for delicious instant sandwiches.
- Cooked pasta and rice freeze well – reheat in minutes in the microwave and save time on busy nights.
- Evaporated milk, available as full-cream or skim milk, is a terrific standby when there is no fresh cream. It can be used for sauces and quiches and it whips well when chilled. Store a few cans in the pantry for emergencies.

VEGETABLE	SERVING SIZE	FIBER CONTENT*
Asparagus, boiled	6–8 spears (60g/2 oz)	1.4
Beans, green, raw	½ cup (6g/½ oz)	1.2
Bean sprouts	2 tbsps (10g/⅓ oz)	0.3
Beets, canned	2 slices (20g/⅔ oz)	0.6
Broccoli, boiled	⅔ cup (100g/3½ oz)	3.9
Cabbage, boiled	½ cup (50g/1¾ oz)	1.0
Carrot, peeled, boiled	1 carrot (100g/3½ oz)	2.9
Cauliflower, boiled	⅔ cup (100g/3½ oz)	2.0
Celery, raw	1 stalk (100g/3½ oz)	0.8
Corn	½ cup kernels (70g/2⅓ oz)	3.5
Cucumber, peeled, raw	4–5 slices (20g/⅔ oz)	0.1
Eggplant, baked	½ small (75g/2½ oz)	2.7
Garlic, raw	2 cloves (10g/⅓ oz)	1.7
Green peppers, raw	¼ capsicum (40g/1⅓ oz)	0.5
Jalapeno peppers, raw	2 chillies (5g/⅙ oz)	0.6
Leek, boiled	1 leek (50g/1¾ oz)	1.4
Lettuce	2 leaves (20g/⅔ oz)	0.1
Mushrooms, raw	4–6 mushrooms (75g/2½ oz)	1.4
Olives	3 green (20g/⅔ oz)	0.8
Onion, peeled, raw	1 onion (80g/2⅔ oz)	0.6
Parsley	2 sprigs (2g/⅐ oz)	0.1
Peas, green, boiled	⅓ cup (40g/1⅓ oz)	1.0
Potato, peeled, roasted	1 medium (120g/4 oz)	2.4
Potato, unpeeled, boiled	1 medium (120g/4 oz)	3.0
Pumpkin, peeled, boiled	½ cup (80g/2⅔ oz)	2.4
Radish, raw	2 radishes (10g/1⅓ oz)	0.1
Swiss Chard, boiled	3 stalks (100g/3½ oz)	2.1
Tomato, raw	1 medium (130g/4½ oz)	2.4
Zucchini, boiled	1 medium (110g/4 oz)	1.5

*grams of dietary fiber per serving

Appetizers

Appetizers, starters, finger food…whatever you call them, they are everybody's favorite course. The best appetizers are not meant to replace your meal, but whet your appetite for what's to come. We've gathered plenty of no-cook options as well the ones meant to impress. Dig into a satisfying dip, tasty tart or crusty bruschetta, and you'll be feasting with your eyes, too.

Onion Pesto Tarts

1 package puff pastry sheets (thawed)
1 tablespoon extra virgin olive oil
2–3 red onions, thinly sliced
salt and freshly ground black pepper
½ teaspoon red pepper flake
2 tablespoons prepared pesto
¼ cup pine nuts

1 Preheat oven to 430°F/220°C. On a floured surface, gently roll out one puff pastry sheet to smooth out the folds. Using a small plate, trace a 4–5 in/10–12½cm circle in the dough and place on a parchment lined baking sheet. With a sharp knife, gently score a ½ in/15mm border inside the circle, but do not cut all the way through the dough. This will form a rim when baked. Repeat with three more tarts.

2 In a large skillet, heat the oil over medium heat. Add onions and season with salt and pepper. Cook for five minutes, stirring occasionally so the onions do not brown on the edges, but soften and deepen in color. Add red pepper flakes and remove from heat.

3 Spread ½ tablespoon of pesto on each pastry round, leaving the border. Spoon onion mixture on top, and scatter with 1 tablespoon of pine nuts. Repeat with remaining rounds.

4 Bake for 12–15 minutes, until the pastry has risen and is golden brown.

Store-bought pesto and frozen puff pastry sheets are delicious and great to keep on hand. The best way to thaw puff pastry is to leave them in the refrigerator overnight.

Serves 4 • Preparation 20 minutes • Cooking 20 minutes

Grilled Vegetable Bruschetta

1 red or yellow pepper, sliced into strips
1 zucchini, halved and thinly sliced lengthwise
1 red onion, halved and thinly sliced crosswise
2 Roma or plum tomatoes, thickly sliced
3 tablespoons extra virgin olive oil
2 teaspoons whole grain mustard
freshly ground black pepper
1 ciabatta loaf, cut into 8 slices, or 8 slices from a baguette
1 clove garlic, halved
8 pitted black olives, thinly sliced
fresh basil to garnish

1 Preheat the grill to high and line the grill rack with foil. Place the pepper, zucchini, onion and tomatoes in a bowl. Whisk together 2 tablespoons of oil, the mustard and black pepper, then pour over the vegetables and toss gently to coat.

2 Spread the vegetables in a single layer on the grill rack and grill for 3–4 minutes on each side, until lightly browned. Set aside and keep warm.

3 Toast the bread slices on both sides under the grill and, while still hot, rub the garlic halves over one side of each piece of toast. Divide the vegetables among the toast slices, piling them onto the garlic side. Scatter over the olives, drizzle over the remaining oil and garnish with fresh basil and serve.

Serves 4 • Preparation 20 minutes • Cooking 10 minutes

Bubble and Squeak

675g/24 oz potatoes, peeled and cut into even-sized pieces
1 clove garlic, peeled
125g/4 oz cabbage, finely sliced
4 green onions, finely sliced
sea salt and freshly ground black pepper
30g/1 oz butter
1 tablespoon canola or vegetable oil

Red Onion Chutney
2 large red onions, finely chopped
60g/2 oz brown sugar
1 tablespoon white wine vinegar

1 Place the potatoes and garlic in a saucepan and cover with water. Bring to a boil, cover and simmer for 15–20 minutes, until tender. Drain, and allow to sit uncovered for 5 minutes, return to the pan and mash until smooth. Cool.

2 Meanwhile, place the cabbage in a saucepan and pour over boiling water to just cover, bring back to the boil, then drain. Add the cabbage, green onions and seasoning to the potato and mix well.

3 Place all the ingredients for the chutney in a saucepan and bring to a boil over a low heat. Simmer uncovered for about 20 minutes, or until almost all of the liquid has evaporated.

4 Divide the potato mixture into eight portions and shape into patties. Melt the butter and oil in a frying pan and fry the cakes over a medium heat for 5 minutes. Turn over, taking care as the cakes are quite soft, and cook for a further 5 minutes, until golden and heated through. Serve with the chutney.

Bubble and Squeak is a traditional English dish that was made with leftover potatoes and vegetables, like a vegetable hash. We've fried them into cakes and serve with a delicious red onion chutney, but you can try it with anything—carrots, brussel sprouts, or zucchini.

Serves 4 • Preparation 25 minutes • Cooking 1 hour

Ricotta Herb Dip with Garlic Toasts

6 pitted green olives, finely chopped
1 tablespoon fresh tarragon, chopped
1 tablespoon fresh chives, chopped
1 tablespoon fresh mint, chopped
finely grated zest of 1 lemon
250g/8 oz ricotta cheese
freshly ground black pepper
4 tablespoons finely chopped sun-dried tomato
1 large baguette, cut into 1cm-thick slices
1 clove garlic, halved

1 Preheat broiler.
2 Mix together the olives, tarragon, chives, mint and lemon zest, then stir in the ricotta. Season with pepper and mix well. Lightly stir the sun-dried tomatoes into the ricotta mixture to create a marbled effect, then spoon into a serving dish.
3 Toast the baguette slices on both sides, until golden. While still hot, rub garlic halves over one side of each piece of toast and serve with the dip.

Serves 4 • Preparation 10 minutes • Cooking 5 minutes

Bruschetta with Goat Cheese and Tomatoes

450g/15 oz small vine-ripened tomatoes
2 tablespoons extra virgin olive oil
1 clove garlic, crushed
4 sprigs fresh thyme
4 thick slices ciabatta, cut on the diagonal
4 tablespoons tapenade, or olive spread
100g/3½ oz goat cheese, cut into chunks
fresh basil leaves to garnish

1 Preheat the oven to 430°F/220°C. Divide the tomatoes into 4 portions of roughly the same size, each still attached to part of the vine and carefully place in a roasting tin, drizzle with the oil and scatter over the garlic and thyme sprigs. Roast for 10 minutes or until the tomatoes are tender.

2 Preheat broiler. Toast the bread on both sides until golden. Spread each slice with 1 tablespoon of tapenade, add a few chunks of goat's cheese and top with the tomatoes on the vine. Drizzle over the juices from the roasting tin and sprinkle with the basil leaves.

There is something so beautiful and rustic about tomatoes on the vine. If you can't find them, juicy cherry or grape tomatoes work just as well in this recipe.

Serves 4 • Preparation 10 minutes • Cooking 15 minutes

Vegetable Tempura

2 eggs
½ cup all-purpose flour, sifted
1 cup canned cranberry sauce
¼ cup orange juice
vegetable oil, for deep-frying
1 zucchini, cut into thick slices
1 large red onion, cut into wedges
225g/1 cup broccoli, cut into small florets
1 red pepper, cut into strips
125g/½ cup green beans, trimmed
125g/½ cup asparagus, trimmed
sea salt
fresh basil leaves, to garnish

1 To make the batter, lightly whisk together the eggs and ¼ cup ice-cold water, then pour on to the flour all at once and whisk quickly, until the batter is smooth.
2 Combine cranberry sauce and orange juice and heat in a small saucepan, over a gentle heat, until warm and runny. Remove from the heat and place in a bowl.
3 Heat 5cm of oil in a wok or frying pan. Dip the vegetables into the batter and coat well. Test the temperature of the oil by dropping in a little batter, if it floats straight back to the surface the oil is hot enough.
4 Deep-fry the vegetables in small batches for 3–4 minutes or until crisp and golden. Remove with a slotted spoon and drain on paper towel. Season with salt. Deep-fry the basil leaves for 20 seconds, until crisp. Serve the vegetables immediately with the cranberry and orange sauce.

Serves 4 • Preparation 25 minutes • Cooking 20 minutes

Cheesy Mushroom Toasts

500g/1 lb assorted fresh wild mushrooms
2 tablespoons olive oil
salt and freshly ground black pepper
30g/1 oz butter
1 clove garlic, crushed
3 tablespoons fresh parsley, chopped
3 tablespoons chives, chopped plus extra whole chives to garnish
2 teaspoons sherry vinegar or balsamic vinegar
⅓ cup soft, spreadable cheese (such as Boursin or Alouette)
3 English Muffins

1 Halve any large mushrooms. Heat 2 teaspoons of the oil in a heavy-based frying pan until smoking, then add the mushrooms, taking care not to crowd the pan. Season and fry over a high heat for 5 minutes, or until they start to release their juices. Remove the mushrooms and drain on paper towel, then set aside, continue until all the mushrooms are cooked.

2 Add the rest of the oil and half the butter to the pan and heat until the butter melts. Add the garlic and stir for 1 minute.

3 Return the mushrooms to the pan, then increase the heat to high and fry for 5 minutes or until they are tender and starting to crisp. Stir in the remaining butter and 2 tablespoons each of parsley and chives, drizzle with the vinegar and season.

4 Mix the soft cheese with the remaining parsley and chives. Split and toast the muffins. Spread the soft cheese mixture over the muffin halves and place on serving plates. Top with the mushrooms and garnish with the whole chives.

Serves 6 • Preparation 25 minutes • Cooking 20 minutes

Potato Croquettes

½ cup long-grain rice
2 large potatoes, cut into chunks
salt and freshly ground black pepper
2 red onions, finely chopped
1 clove garlic, crushed
⅓ cup fresh parsley, chopped
½ cup sesame seeds
canola or vegetable oil for frying

1 Combine the rice with ¾ cup water in a saucepan. Bring to a boil, reduce heat to low, cover and cook for 15 minutes. Remove pan from heat and spread on a plate. Leave for 1 hour or until cooled completely, fluffing it up with a fork occasionally.

2 Meanwhile put the potatoes into a large saucepan of boiling salted water and simmer for 15–20 minutes, until tender. Drain, mash and combine the mashed potato with the cooled rice, seasoning, onions, garlic and parsley. Mix thoroughly.

3 Shape the mixture into 8 croquettes with your hands, then roll in the sesame seeds. Heat 1cm of oil in a large, heavy-based frying pan and fry the croquettes for 2–3 minutes, turning constantly until crisp and browned all over.

Serves 4 • Preparation 20 minutes • Cooking 45 minutes

Fried Zucchini Fennel Cakes

⅔ cup flour
1 egg, separated
1 tablespoon olive oil
¼ teaspoon salt and freshly ground black pepper
1 medium fennel bulb
1 large zucchini
1 tablespoon mint, chopped
vegetable oil, for shallow frying
250g/8 oz tzaziki

1 Sift the flour into a bowl and make a well. Into the well add the egg until a smooth batter has formed. Season with salt and pepper, cover and leave to thicken for 30 minutes in a cool place.

2 Grate the fennel and zucchini and stir the chopped mint into the batter. Whisk the egg white until soft peaks form and fold gently into the batter mixture.

3 Place a heavy-based frying pan over a medium heat and lightly coat with oil. Using a tablespoon, add measured amounts of mixture to the pan, a few at a time. When golden, turn and cook on the other side. Repeat until all the mixture has been used. Drain on paper towel and serve warm with tzaziki.

These crispy veggie cakes are delicious plain, or with tzatziki dip. You can purchase it or make your own by combining greek yogurt, grated cucumber, garlic, salt, pepper and a squeeze of lemon juice.

Serves 6 • Preparation 35 minutes • Cooking 20 minutes

Spiced Olives

500g/1 lb green or black olives
1 sprig fresh oregano
1 sprig fresh thyme
1 teaspoon fresh rosemary, chopped
2 bay leaves
1 teaspoon fennel seeds, bruised
1 teaspoon cumin seeds, bruised
1 fresh red chilli, deseeded and chopped
4 cloves garlic, crushed

1 Using a small sharp knife make a lengthwise slit through to the pit of each olive. Combine the olives with the remaining ingredients and mix well. Pack the mixture into a jar with enough oil to cover. Seal and leave at least 3 days, shaking jar occasionally.

Serves 6 • Preparation 10 minutes

Spinach and Goat Cheese Pizza

125g/4 oz sun-dried tomatoes in oil, drained, plus 2 tablespoons oil from the jar
2 tablespoons tomato paste
1 clove garlic, roughly chopped
2 teaspoons fresh thyme, finely chopped
250g/8 oz baby spinach
6 mini pita breads
6 cherry tomatoes, quartered
100g/3½ oz goat cheese, crumbled
1 tablespoon sesame seeds

1 Preheat the oven to 450°F/230°C. Purée the sun-dried tomatoes, tomato paste and garlic in a food processor or with a hand blender. Mix in the thyme.

2 Bring a pan of water to the boil, immerse the spinach then remove and refresh in a bowl of cold water. Drain, then drizzle the sun-dried tomato oil over the top.

3 Spread the tomato and garlic purée over the pita breads and top with the spinach. Scatter with cherry tomatoes, cheese and sesame seeds. Cook for 10 minutes or until the cheese has melted slightly and started to brown.

Serves 4 • Preparation 15 minutes • Cooking 10 minutes

Hummus

400g/14 oz canned chickpeas, drained and rinsed
juice of 1 lemon
¼ cup extra virgin olive oil
2 tablespoons tahini
1 clove garlic, crushed
½ teaspoon ground cilantro
½ teaspoon ground cumin
freshly ground black pepper
500g/1 lb mixed vegetables; choose from red pepper, carrots, zucchini, cauliflower, broccoli, mushrooms, radishes, baby asparagus and green onions

1 In a food processor or with a hand blender, blend the chickpeas, lemon juice, olive oil, tahini, garlic, cilantro, cumin and black pepper until they form a coarse paste.
2 Slice the red pepper, carrots and zucchini into sticks, and cut the cauliflower and broccoli into florets. Wipe the mushrooms and trim the radishes, asparagus and green onions. Arrange the vegetables on a serving plate. Spoon the hummus into a serving bowl and serve with the crudités.

Serves 4 • Preparation 25 minutes

Caramelized Shallot and Asparagus Bruschetta

¼ cup olive oil
300g/10 oz shallots, roughly chopped
2 cloves garlic, thickly sliced
1½ tablespoons brown sugar
2 tablespoons dark soy sauce
1 tablespoon white wine vinegar or cider vinegar
150mL/5 oz white wine
¼ bunch asparagus, tips only
4 Roma or plum tomatoes
juice of ½ lemon
2 medium baguettes, thickly sliced
flat-leaf parsley or cilantro to garnish

1 Heat the oil in a wok or large heavy-based frying pan. Add the shallots, garlic and stir-fry for 4–5 minutes, until they start to color. Add the sugar and the soy sauce and stir-fry for 3–4 minutes, until the shallots are evenly browned.

2 Add the vinegar and wine to the shallots and bring to a boil. Reduce the heat and simmer, uncovered, for 8 minutes, or until the shallots have softened and the liquid has thickened and looks glossy. Add the asparagus tips, cover and cook for 4–5 minutes, stirring occasionally.

3 Place the tomatoes in a bowl and cover with boiling water. Leave for 30 seconds, then peel, remove seeds and chop. Add to the pan with the lemon juice, stir and heat for 1–2 minutes.

4 Preheat broiler. Toast the bread on both sides. Serve the toasts topped with the vegetable mixture and garnished with the parsley or cilantro.

Serves 6 • Preparation 25 minutes • Cooking 30 minutes

Roasted Red Pepper Dip

2 red bell peppers
2 teaspoons cumin seeds
200g/7 oz Greek yogurt
2 tablespoons fresh mint, finely chopped
salt and freshly ground black pepper
1 teaspoon paprika to garnish

1 Preheat broiler. Cut the red bell peppers, lengthwise into quarters, then remove the seeds and grill, skin-side up, for 10 minutes or until blackened and blistered. Place in a plastic bag and leave to cool for 10 minutes.
2 Toast the cumin seeds in a small frying pan, stirring constantly over medium to high heat, until aromatic. Remove and reserve. Peel the skins from the grilled red bell peppers and discard, then roughly chop the flesh.
3 Mix the red bell peppers with the yogurt, cumin seeds and mint and season to taste. Transfer to a serving dish and garnish with the paprika.

Serves 4 • Preparation 25 minutes • Cooking 10 minutes

Soups

Whether you're in the mood for a luxurious, creamy soup or a thick, chunky soup brimming with vegetables, soups are quite possibly the perfect meal. They're easy to cook and produce results that everyone loves. Most of these recipes take minutes, not hours, so try making a big batch for easy meals throughout the week.

Avocado Gazpacho

2 large ripe avocados, peeled and chopped
grated zest and juice of 1 lemon
600mL/21 oz vegetable stock
2 large tomatoes
1 medium cucumber, chopped
1 green and 1 red bell pepper, seeded and chopped
1 clove garlic, crushed
salt and freshly ground black pepper
⅓ cup chives, chopped

1 Place the avocados, lemon zest, juice and stock in a food processor and
  blend until smooth. Pour into a large bowl and set aside.

2 Place the tomatoes in a bowl, cover with boiling water and leave for
  30 seconds. Remove from the bowl, peel off the skins, remove the seeds
  and chop the flesh. Reserve a little chopped tomato and cucumber for the
  garnish. Place the rest of the tomatoes and cucumber in the food processor
  with the peppers, garlic and seasoning and blend to a purée.

3 Add the tomato mixture to the avocado purée, mixing thoroughly. Cover
  and refrigerate for 1 hour. Serve garnished with chives, the reserved
  tomato and cucumber.

Serves 4 • Preparation 20 minutes + 1 hour cooling

Fresh Pea Soup

60g/2 oz butter
bunch of green onions, chopped
1 vegetable bouillon cube, crumbled
450g/15 oz shelled fresh peas, or frozen peas
1 Romaine heart, shredded
salt and freshly ground black pepper
½ bunch fresh mint, chopped
½ cup heavy cream
pinch of sugar
fresh lemon juice
thickened cream to serve and chopped fresh chives to garnish

1 Melt the butter in a large heavy-based saucepan. Add the green onions, bouillon cube, cover and cook gently for 2 minutes.
2 Add the peas and lettuce and 3½ cups of water. Season well, bring to a boil, then simmer for 10 minutes or until the vegetables are tender. Purée with the mint and cream until smooth, using a food processor or a hand blender.
3 Return the soup to the pan. Season again, if necessary, then add the sugar and lemon juice, if using. Reheat gently but do not allow the soup to boil. Serve with a dollop of crème fraiche and garnish of chopped chives.

Serves 4 • Preparation 20 minutes • Cooking 20 minutes

Cumin-Spiced Carrot Soup

1 tablespoon olive oil
1 large onion, chopped
1 clove garlic, crushed
3 stalks celery, chopped
1 tablespoon ground cumin
6 medium carrots, thinly sliced
3½ cups vegetable stock
freshly ground black pepper
fresh cilantro to garnish

1 Heat the oil in a large saucepan, add the onion, garlic and celery and fry gently for 5 minutes or until softened, stirring occasionally. Add the cumin and fry, stirring, for 1 minute to release its flavor.

2 Add the carrots, stock and black pepper to the onion mixture and stir to combine. Bring to a simmer, cover and stir occasionally, for 30–35 minutes, until the vegetables are tender.

3 Remove the pan from the heat and cool for a few minutes. Purée the soup until smooth in a food processor, or with a hand blender. Return to a clean pan and reheat gently. Serve garnished with fresh cilantro.

Serves 4 • Preparation 20 minutes • Cooking 45 minutes

Spinach Soup with Cheese Toasts

2 tablespoons olive oil
30g/1 oz butter
250g/8 oz russet or Idaho potatoes, cut into 1 in/25mm cubes
250g/8 oz spinach leaves
1 teaspoon freshly grated nutmeg
50mL/5 oz vegetable stock
salt and freshly ground black pepper
½ cup crème fraîche
100g/3½ oz Gruyère or Cheddar cheese, grated
1 large egg, beaten
French bread, cut diagonally into 18 slices

1 Heat the oil and half the butter in a large saucepan. Sauté the potatoes for
   1 minute, then add the spinach and the nutmeg. Cook for 2 minutes or until
   the spinach is wilted.

2 Add the stock to the potato and spinach mixture, season lightly and bring
   to a boil. Reduce the heat, cover and simmer for 10–15 minutes, until the
   potatoes are tender. Let cool for 10 minutes.

3 Pour the soup into a food processor and blend until smooth. Alternatively,
   use a hand blender. Stir in half the crème fraîche, then adjust the seasoning
   to taste. Set aside.

4 Preheat the broiler. Mix the grated cheese with the egg and the rest of the
   crème fraîche. Lightly toast the bread slices, then spread the cheese mixture
   over one side of each slice. Dot with the rest of the butter and season with a
   little black pepper. Broil for 1–2 minutes or until bubbling and golden. Heat
   the soup through and serve topped with the cheese toasts.

Serves 6 • Preparation 30 minutes • Cooking 25 minutes

Vegetable Soup

2 tablespoons olive oil
1 onion, finely chopped
2 cloves garlic, crushed
1 potato, finely diced
1 carrot, finely diced
2 teaspoon cumin seeds
3½ cups vegetable stock
2 stalks celery, finely chopped
1 large zucchini, finely chopped
125g/4 oz green beans, cut into 25mm pieces
420g/15 oz canned butter beans, drained
400g/14 oz canned chopped tomatoes
freshly ground black pepper
60g/2 oz Cheddar cheese, grated

1 Heat the oil in a large heavy-based saucepan, then add the onion, garlic, potato,
   carrot and cumin seeds. Cook, uncovered, for 5 minutes, stirring from time to time,
   until the vegetables have softened.

2 Add the stock, celery and zucchini and bring to a simmer for 10 minutes, or until the
   celery and zucchini are tender.

3 Stir in the green beans, butter beans, chopped tomatoes and plenty of seasoning.
   Simmer, uncovered, for 5 minutes or until the green beans are tender. Pour the soup
   into bowls and top with the grated Cheddar.

Serves 4 • Preparation 20 minutes • Cooking 25 minutes

Sweet Potato Soup

30g/1 oz butter
450g/15 oz sweet potatoes, cut into ¼ in/12mm dice
1 onion, chopped
2 cloves garlic, crushed
1 teaspoon grated ginger
1 tablespoon red curry paste
600mL/24 oz vegetable stock
200mL/7 oz coconut milk
juice of 1 lime
¼ teaspoon red pepper flakes
150g/5 oz fresh spinach, shredded
salt and freshly ground black pepper

1 Melt the butter in a saucepan and sauté the potatoes, onion, garlic, ginger and curry paste for 5 minutes or until lightly golden.

2 Add the stock, coconut milk, lime juice and red pepper flakes. Bring to a boil, cover and simmer for 15 minutes or until the potatoes are tender.

3 When the soup is slightly cooled, puree half of it in a food processor or with a hand blender. Return the pureed soup to the pan, add the spinach and cook for 1–2 minutes, until the spinach has just wilted and the soup has heated through. Season to taste.

Serves 4 • Preparation 30 minutes • Cooking 25 minutes

Indian-Spiced Potato Soup

1 tablespoon vegetable oil
1 onion, finely chopped
1cm piece ginger, finely chopped
2 large potatoes, cut into ½ in/1cm cubes
2 teaspoons ground cumin
2 teaspoons ground cilantro
½ teaspoon turmeric
1 teaspoon ground cinnamon
4 cups vegetable stock
salt and freshly ground black pepper
1 tablespoon natural yogurt to garnish

1 Heat the oil in a large saucepan. Fry the onion and ginger for 5 minutes or until
   softened. Add the potatoes and sauté for another minute, stirring often.

2 Mix the cumin, cilantro, turmeric and cinnamon with 2 tablespoons of cold water
   to make a paste. Add to the onion and potato, stirring well, and fry for 1 minute
   or until aromatic.

3 Add the stock and season to taste. Bring to a boil, then reduce the heat, cover
   and simmer for 30 minutes or until the potato is tender. Blend until smooth in a
   food processor, or press through a metal sieve. Return to the pan and gently heat
   through. Garnish with the yogurt and more black pepper.

Serves 4 • Preparation 25 minutes • Cooking 40 minutes

Minestrone with Pesto

¼ cup olive oil
1 onion, chopped
2 cloves garlic, chopped
1 potato, cut into 1cm cubes
2 small carrots, cut into 1cm cubes
1 large zucchini, cut into 1cm cubes
¼ cabbage, chopped
3 cups vegetable stock
800g/28 oz canned chopped tomatoes
75g/2½ oz pasta shapes, such as shells
salt and freshly ground black pepper
4 tablespoons pesto
4 tablespoons grated Parmesan

1 Place the oil in a large heavy-based saucepan, then add the onion, garlic, potato, carrots, zucchini and cabbage and cook for 5–7 minutes, until slightly softened.

2 Add the stock and tomatoes and bring to a boil. Reduce the heat and simmer for 20 minutes, then add the pasta shapes and seasoning and cook for a further 15 minutes, or until the pasta is tender but still firm to the bite. Divide the soup among bowls and top each serving with a tablespoon of pesto and sprinkle with Parmesan.

Serves 4 • Preparation 20 minutes • Cooking 45 minutes

Roasted Red Pepper Soup

3 red or orange bell peppers, halved and cored
1 onion, unpeeled and halved
4 large Roma or plum tomatoes
4 cloves garlic, unpeeled
350mL/12 oz vegetable stock
1 tablespoon tomato purée
salt and freshly ground black pepper
¼ bunch fresh parsley, chopped

1 Preheat the oven to 400°F/200°C. Place the peppers and onion on a baking sheet, cut-side down, and add the whole tomatoes and garlic. Cook in the oven for 30 minutes or until tender and well browned.

2 Leave the vegetables and garlic to cool for 10 minutes, then peel. Place the vegetables and garlic in a food processor with half the stock and blend until smooth. Alternatively use a hand blender.

3 Return to the pan, add the remaining stock and the tomato purée, then bring to a boil. Season to taste and scatter with parsley just before serving.

Serves 4 • Preparation 25 minutes • Cooking 50 minutes

Tuscan Bean Soup

½ loaf ciabatta, preferably a day or two old
¼ cup olive oil
3 onions, chopped
3 cloves garlic, chopped
800g/28 oz canned chopped tomatoes
400g/14 oz canned white beans
600mL/200 oz vegetable stock
salt and freshly ground black pepper
fresh basil to garnish

1 Preheat the oven to 300°F/150°C. Cut the ciabatta into dice, then place in the oven for 10 minutes to dry out.

2 Heat the olive oil in a large saucepan, add the onions and garlic, and cook for 3–4 minutes, until soft. Add the tomatoes, beans and stock. Bring to a boil, then simmer for 2 minutes.

3 Stir in the diced ciabatta, bring the soup back to the boil, then simmer for a further 5 minutes. Season and serve garnished with basil.

Serves 4 • Preparation 20 minutes • Cooking 25 minutes

Cream of Mushroom Soup with Crispy Onions

30g/1 oz butter
1 tablespoon extra virgin olive oil
4 green onions, chopped
375g/13 oz mushrooms, sliced
1 medium potato, peeled and chopped
3½ cups vegetable stock
sea salt and freshly ground black pepper
⅓ cup heavy cream
juice of ½ lemon
chopped fresh parsley, to garnish

Crispy onions
canola or vegetable oil, for frying
1 large onion, finely sliced into rings
1 tablespoon flour

1 Heat the butter and oil in a large saucepan and fry the green onions and mushrooms over a medium to high heat for 5 minutes, until softened and most of the juices have evaporated.

2 Add the potato, vegetable stock and seasoning and bring to a boil. Reduce the heat, cover and simmer for 20 minutes until the potatoes are tender. Allow to cool.

3 Heat about 1cm oil in a frying pan. Coat the onions in the flour, add to the pan and cook for 5 minutes or until crisp and lightly golden. Drain on paper towel.

4 Purée the soup in a food processor or hand blender and return to the saucepan. Stir in the cream and lemon juice and gently reheat. Ladle the soup into bowls and top with the crispy onions. Sprinkle with chopped fresh parsley and serve.

Serves 4 • Preparation 25 minutes • Cooking 40 minutes

Carrot Lentil Soup

30g/1 oz butter
1 tablespoon canola or vegetable oil
450g/15 oz carrots, chopped
1 onion, chopped
2 stalks celery, chopped
100g/3½ oz split red lentils, rinsed
3⅓ cups vegetable stock
sea salt and freshly ground black pepper
plain or Greek yogurt and chopped fresh parsley, to garnish

1 Melt the butter with the oil in a saucepan and fry the carrots, onion and celery for 6–8 minutes or until lightly golden. Add the lentils and 3 cups of vegetable stock and bring to a boil. Cover and simmer for about 20 minutes, until the carrots are tender.

2 Allow the soup to cool for about 15 minutes, then purée until smooth in food processor or blender. Return to a clean saucepan with the remaining stock, add seasoning to taste and reheat gently before serving. Add a swirl of yogurt and a sprinkling of chopped fresh parsley to garnish.

Serves 4 • Preparation 20 minutes • Cooking 45 minutes

Roasted Tomato Soup with Chickpeas

500g/1 lb dried chickpeas
1kg/2 lb Roma or plum tomatoes
1 bulb garlic
⅓ cup olive oil
2 tablespoons dried oregano
2 leeks, sliced, white part only
4 cups vegetable stock
2 tablespoons tomato paste
salt and pepper
fresh oregano leaves

1   Soak chickpeas in cold water overnight. Drain and place chickpeas in a saucepan
    covered with water and bring to a boil, then simmer for approximately one hour
    until chickpeas are cooked. Drain and set aside.

2   Preheat the oven to 400°F/200°C. Halve the tomatoes and place them on a baking
    tray. Cut the top off the garlic bulb and place on the baking sheet, drizzle with
    a little olive oil, sprinkle with salt and dried oregano, and roast in the oven for
    20–30 minutes.

3   Place the tomatoes and five peeled garlic cloves (reserve the rest) in a food
    processor, and purée for one minute. Heat half the remaining oil and sauté
    the leeks for 3 minutes, add the stock, and bring to a boil, then reduce heat to
    simmer. Add the tomato mixture, tomato paste and the chickpeas, season with
    salt and pepper, and heat through. Sprinkle with fresh oregano leaves.

Serves 4 • Preparation 25 minutes • Cooking 2 hours

Salads

Salads aren't just a light side dish—they can be a full meal. And few meals are quicker to make. We've pulled together our favorite tossed green salads, composed salads, warm salads, as well as grains. Great salads have just the right amount of dressing—just enough to cling to the ingredients. For the crispest and freshest salads, always add the dressing at the last minute.

Celery, Carrot and Apple Salad

3 carrots, grated
1 celery heart, thinly sliced
2 eating apples, peeled, cored and thinly sliced

Dressing
3 tablespoons lemon juice
1 clove garlic, crushed
2 tablespoons tahini

1 To make the dressing, place the lemon juice, garlic, tahini and 3 tablespoons of water in a food processor and blend until smooth. Alternatively, combine with a fork. Season to taste.

2 Toss together the carrots, celery heart and apples and transfer to individual serving bowls. Drizzle over the dressing.

Serves 4 • Preparation 10 minutes • Cooking none

Roasted Beet Salad

24 baby or 12 large beets, with greens attached if possible
1 tablespoon olive oil
salt and freshly ground pepper to taste
1 tablespoon butter
2 tablespoons balsamic vinegar
1 bunch fresh dill, chopped
100g/3½ oz hazelnuts, roasted and chopped
2 tablespoons sour cream or Greek yogurt (optional)
freshly ground black pepper to taste

1 Preheat oven to 400°F/200°C.

2 If your beets have their greens attached, remove them and set the greens aside.
   Wash the beets and scrub them until clean. Trim the bottom if necessary but be
   careful not to cut the beet itself. Toss the beets and olive oil together then place
   in a baking dish. Cover with foil or a lid and roast for 30–45 minutes or until tender.

3 Remove the beets from the oven and cool then peel the skin away and discard. Cut
   the beets in half lengthwise and season. Meanwhile, wash the greens thoroughly to
   remove all traces of sand and grit. Heat the butter in a sauté pan and add the beet
   greens, tossing for 1 minute until wilted. Remove, add the balsamic vinegar and
   bring to a boil. Whisk in the butter and return the peeled beets and toss them in the
   balsamic. Continue until reduced and shiny.

4 Serve with the wilted beet leaves. Scatter over the dill and roasted hazelnuts, adding
   small dollops of the sour cream or yogurt if desired. Add black pepper to taste.

Serves 4 • Preparation 35 minutes • Cooking 1 hour 10 minutes

Endive Salad with Apples, Blue Cheese and Pecans

5 heads Belgian endive
1 red delicious apple, cored, quartered
1 Granny Smith apple, cored, quartered
lemon juice
200g/7 oz arugula
1 cup coarsely chopped pecans, toasted
100g/3½ oz crumbled blue cheese such as Gorgonzola

Dressing
¼ cup olive oil
¼ cup walnut oil
¼ cup sherry vinegar
1 large shallot, minced
salt and pepper to taste

1 Cut the endive in half, lengthwise then lay the endive cut-side down on a board and cut the leaves into thin strips. Thinly slice the unpeeled apples and toss with the lemon juice. Wash the rocket leaves and drain well.

2 Combine endive strips, apple slices, arugula, toasted pecans and blue cheese in a large bowl.

3 Whisk the oils, vinegar and shallot in small bowl then season to taste with salt and pepper. Drizzle the dressing over the salad and toss thoroughly. Serve immediately.

Serves 4 • Preparation 20 minutes • Cooking none

Oven Roasted Tomato and Eggplant

3 small eggplants
4–5 Roma or plum tomatoes
2 cloves garlic, minced
1 tablespoon olive oil
10 basil leaves
2 tablespoons fresh rosemary, finely chopped
60g/2 oz feta cheese, crumbled
salt and freshly ground black pepper
basil sprigs to garnish

1 Halve the eggplants lengthwise then cut into 1 in/25mm slices, lengthwise. Sprinkle with salt and allow to rest for 30 minutes, rinse and dry thoroughly.

2 Slice the tomatoes lengthwise. Mix the minced garlic with the olive oil and set aside. Place the eggplant on non-stick oven trays with a slice of tomato in between every 2 slices of eggplant. Tear the basil leaves and insert between the tomato and eggplant. Brush with garlic oil and sprinkle with rosemary.

3 Preheat the oven to 480°F/250°. Brush the garlic oil over the eggplant and sprinkle with finely chopped rosemary. Bake the eggplant fans for 15 minutes then remove from the oven. Crumble the feta cheese over the eggplant fans, add salt and black pepper to taste. Return to the oven until the cheese browns slightly.

4 Garnish with extra basil sprigs and black pepper, drizzle with extra olive oil and serve immediately.

Serves 2 • Preparation 50 minutes • Cooking 15 minutes

Quick Tabouli

1 cup quick-cooking barley
⅓ cup parsley, finely chopped
2 tablespoons mint, finely chopped
1 bunch green onions (include some of the green tops), finely chopped
2 tomatoes, chopped
1 red or green bell pepper, finely diced
⅓ cup olive oil
2 tablespoons lemon juice
½ teaspoon salt
freshly ground black pepper

1 Cook the barley in a large saucepan with 4 cups of boiling salted water, stirring.
   Cook until tender, about 15 minutes. Drain in a colander and rinse under running
   water. Drain thoroughly.
2 Place barley in a bowl with parsley, mint, green onions, tomatoes and capsicum.
   Mix together the oil, lemon juice, salt and freshly ground pepper. Add to salad,
   toss to mix. Refrigerate before serving.

**Traditional Tabouli is made with bulgar, or cracked wheat, but quick cooking barley
makes a great substitute. It's great on its own, with pita bread, or stuffed into
peppers or lettuce leaves.**

Serves 4 • Preparation 15 minutes • Cooking 15 minutes

Artichokes Braised in White Wine

6 globe artichokes
2 tablespoons olive oil
1 small onion, peeled and finely chopped
2 cloves garlic, peeled and finely sliced
200mL/7 oz white wine or dry sherry
salt
freshly grated nutmeg

1 Remove stems and tough outer leaves from the artichokes. Wash well and cut each into quarters, lengthwise.

2 In a large pan, heat the oil and gently sauté the onion and garlic for about 4 minutes. Add the artichokes and wine, season with salt and nutmeg.

3 Cover and cook on medium low heat for 20-40 minutes depending on size. Test by pulling a leaf; if done, it will pull away easily. If the liquid reduces too much, add a little water.

Serves 4 • Preparation 20 minutes • Cooking 40 minutes

Crunchy Lentil Salad

1 cup brown lentils
1½ cups crunchy fresh small bean sprouts or alfalfa sprouts
½ cup fresh mint, coarsely chopped
½ red onion, finely chopped
¼ cup fresh orange juice
2 tablespoons extra virgin olive oil
1 tablespoon balsamic or wine vinegar
1 teaspoon grated orange zest
1 teaspoon ground cumin
1 teaspoon salt
freshly ground black pepper, to taste

1　Bring a saucepan of lightly salted water to a boil and add the lentils. Reduce the heat and simmer until just tender, about 30 minutes.

2　Drain the lentils, rinse under cold water and pat dry. Place lentils in a salad bowl and add all the remaining ingredients. Toss well to combine. Cover and refrigerate for several hours before serving.

Serves 4–6 • Preparation 20 minutes • Cooking 35 minutes

Eggplant Salad

1 large eggplant, cubed
¼ cup vegetable oil
2 cloves garlic
¼ cup red wine vinegar
⅓ cup olive oil
⅓ cup chopped parsley
chopped basil leaves or dill to taste
1 red bell pepper
1 green onion, finely chopped

1 Heat oil in a pan over medium-low heat and add eggplant. Cover and cook, stirring regularly until pale golden and tender. Allow to cool in a colander to drain excess oil. Meanwhile in a food processor purée the garlic with the vinegar, olive oil, herbs, salt and pepper to taste.

2 Toss the eggplant in the dressing in serving bowl. Char the red pepper over a gas flame on under a hot broiler until skin is blackened and blistered all over. Place pepper in bowl and cover tightly with plastic wrap. After several minutes the blackened skin will peel off easily. Peel pepper and remove core and seeds. Cut into large chunks and toss into the salad. Garnish with chopped red onion.

Serves 4 • Preparation 35 minutes • Cooking 20 minutes

Aïoli with Veggies

4 cloves garlic
½ teaspoon salt
2 egg yolks
½ teaspoon Dijon mustard
freshly ground black pepper
lemon juice to taste
1¼ cups olive oil

1 Peel the garlic and crush with the flat of a knife. Sprinkle with the salt and still using the knife, work to a smooth paste. Mix in a bowl with the egg yolks, mustard, pepper and lemon juice.

2 Using a wire whisk, gradually add oil in slow stream, whisking constantly, until a quarter cup has been added. Continue adding the rest of the oil in a thin stream, whisking to incorporate it into a creamy, thick mayonnaise.

3 Serve with a selection of fresh vegetables such as lettuces, peapods, zucchini, green onions, radishes, beans, celery, carrots, boiled potatoes, or hard-boiled eggs.

Serves 4 • Preparation 30 minutes • Cooking none

Pear and Watercress Salad

125g/4 oz goat cheese, crumbled
1 tablespoon heavy cream
½ bunch watercress leaves, finely chopped
¼ bunch parsley leaves, chopped
2 tablespoons toasted walnuts, chopped
salt and freshly ground black pepper
4 ripe pears
juice of 1 lemon
1 bunch watercress, washed and dried thoroughly
2 tablespoons white wine vinegar
½ cup virgin olive oil

1 Combine goat cheese, cream, watercress, parsley, and walnuts. Season with salt
   and pepper and refrigerate.
2 Whisk together white wine vinegar and olive oil, season with salt and pepper
   and reserve.
3 Just before serving, dress the watercress. Cut each pears in half lengthwise and
   hollow out the core. Squeeze lemon juice over the pear and stuff with the goat
   cheese mixture. Cut in half lengthwise and serve with dressed watercress.

Serves 4 • Preparation 15 minutes • Cooking none

Spinach Salad with Mushroom and Parmesan

1 bunch baby spinach
250g/8 oz button mushrooms
1 teaspoon lemon juice or balsamic vinegar
salt and freshly ground black pepper
2 tablespoons extra virgin olive oil
60g/2 oz Parmesan cheese, shaved using a vegetable peeler

1 Thoroughly wash and dry the spinach, then tear into bite-size pieces. If preparing ahead, pack into plastic bags and store in refrigerator until ready.
2 Just before serving, slice button mushrooms thinly, adding them to a bowl with the lemon juice or vinegar.
3 Season and arrange on a platter with the spinach leaves. Drizzle with virgin olive oil, scatter with Parmesan shavings and season well with pepper.

Serves 4 • Preparation 20 minutes • Cooking none

Rice and Pasta

Rice and pasta are fantastic convenience foods, and perfect for the vegetarian lifestyle. They're quick to cook, easy to master, and adaptable to endless variations. Whether you're craving a simple sauce or something more elaborate, these comforting dishes are sure to be crowd pleasers.

Wild Mushroom Risotto

4 cups vegetable stock
2 tablespoons butter
500g/1 lb assorted wild mushrooms, such as cremini, porcini, portabella, oyster or shiitake, sliced
2 tablespoons olive oil
2 cloves garlic, minced
1 leek, finely sliced
2 cups Arborio rice
½ cup white wine
zest of 1 lemon, finely grated
½ cup pecorino cheese, grated
½ cup Parmesan cheese, grated
2 tablespoons parsley, chopped

1 Place stock in a saucepan and bring to a boil. Leave simmering. In a large skillet on medium heat, heat butter, add mushrooms and sauté for a few minutes until slightly browned. Remove from pan and reserve.

2 In the same skillet, heat oil, add garlic, leeks and cook until onions are translucent and leeks are softened, about 5 minutes.

3 Add the rice to the leek and garlic and stir for 1 minute, to coat the rice. Add the white wine, and cook, until liquid is absorbed. Start adding the warm stock, a ladle at a time, stirring continuously, until liquid has been absorbed. Continue adding stock a ladle at a time until stock is used and rice is cooked.

4 Stir in mushrooms, lemon zest, cheese and parsley. Serve immediately.

Serves 4–6 • Preparation 25 minutes • Cooking 40 minutes

Risotto with Spinach and Gorgonzola

4 cups vegetable stock
2 tablespoons olive oil
2 cloves garlic, crushed
1 onion, finely chopped
2 cups Arborio rice
½ cup white wine
150g/5 oz baby spinach
220g/8 oz Gorgonzola cheese, in small pieces
salt and freshly ground black pepper

1 Place stock in a saucepan and bring to a boil. Leave simmering.
2 Heat oil in a large saucepan, add garlic and onion, and cook for 5 minutes, or until soft. Add rice, and stir, until well coated.
3 Pour in wine, and cook, until the liquid has been absorbed. Add a ladle of the stock, stir continuously, until the liquid has been absorbed, then add the next ladle of stock. Keep adding stock this way, and stirring, until all the stock is used, and until the rice is cooked, but still a little firm to bite.
4 Add the spinach, cheese and seasonings. Stir and cook until spinach is just wilted and cheese has melted. Serve immediately.

Serves 6 • Preparation 30 minutes • Cooking 45 minutes

Lemon and Broccoli Risotto

4 cups vegetable stock
1 tablespoon olive oil
1 onion, chopped
1 clove garlic, crushed
1½ cups Arborio rice
1 cup dry white wine
125g/4 oz broccoli florets
½ bunch fresh parsley, chopped
finely grated zest and juice of 1 lemon
crushed black peppercorns

1 Place stock in a saucepan and bring to a boil. Leave simmering. In a large skillet, heat oil over medium heat, add onions and garlic. Cook, stirring, until onion is translucent, about 2 minutes.

2 Stir in rice. Cook for 1–2 minutes. Add wine. Cook, stirring, until liquid is absorbed. Add 1 ladle stock and cook, stirring occasionally until liquid is absorbed. Add another ladle of stock and cook as described above. Continue until all the stock is used and the rice is tender. Add broccoli 2–3 minutes before end of cooking time.

3 Stir in parsley, lemon zest and juice and freshly ground black pepper to taste. Remove pan from heat. Stand for 3 minutes then serve.

Serves 4 • Preparation 25 minutes • Cooking 40 minutes

Asparagus Lemon Risotto

2 tablespoons olive oil
1 onion, chopped
1½ cup Arborio rice
200mL/7 oz white wine
3 cups vegetable stock
100g/3½ oz asparagus tips, cut into bite-size pieces
60g/2 oz butter
75g/2½ oz Parmesan, grated
salt and freshly ground black pepper
2 tablespoons fresh parsley, chopped
finely grated zest of 1 lemon

1 In a pan, gently simmer the stock. Heat the oil in a large, heavy-based saucepan or frying pan, then add the onion and fry for 3–4 minutes, until golden. Add the rice and stir for 1 minute or until coated with the oil. Stir in the wine and bring to a boil, then reduce the heat and continue stirring for 4–5 minutes, until the wine has been absorbed by the rice.

2 Pour about one-third of the stock into the rice and simmer, stirring constantly for 4–5 minutes, until the stock has been absorbed. Add half the remaining stock and cook, stirring, until absorbed. Add the remaining stock and the asparagus and cook, stirring, for 5 minutes or until the rice and asparagus are tender but still firm to the bite.

3 Add the butter and half the Parmesan and season. Cook, stirring constantly, for 1 minute or until the butter and cheese have melted into the rice. Sprinkle with the remaining Parmesan, parsley and lemon zest.

Serves 6 • Preparation 30 minutes • Cooking 45 minutes

Pumpkin Parmesan Risotto

4 cups vegetable stock
large pinch of saffron threads
2 tablespoons olive oil
15g/½ oz butter
1 onion, chopped
1 clove garlic, finely chopped
2 cups Arborio rice
1kg/2 lb pumpkin or butternut squash, peeled, seeded and cut into 1 in/25mm pieces
150mL/5 oz dry white wine
salt and freshly ground black pepper
grated zest and juice of 1 lemon
60g/2 oz Parmesan, grated
1 sprig fresh rosemary, finely chopped

1 Heat 1 cup of the stock in a saucepan until boiling, then remove the pan from the heat and stir in the saffron threads.

2 Heat the oil and butter in a large heavy-based pan and gently fry the onion and garlic for 4–5 minutes, until softened but not browned. Add the rice and pumpkin or squash to the pan, and stir for 2 minutes or until the rice is coated with oil.

3 Stir in the wine and boil for a few seconds to cook off the alcohol, then pour in the saffron stock. Simmer, stirring constantly, for 5 minutes or until the stock has been absorbed. Add half the remaining stock and cook, stirring, for 5 minutes or until absorbed. Add the remaining stock and cook, stirring, for a further 5 minutes or until the rice is tender but still firm to the bite. Season.

4 Stir the lemon zest and juice and the Parmesan into the risotto, then garnish with rosemary.

Serves 4 • Preparation 30 minutes • Cooking 40 minutes

Rice Pilaf with Apricot

3 tablespoons oil or butter
1 large onion, finely chopped
1½ cups rice
3½ cups hot water
salt and freshly ground pepper
2 tablespoons parsley, finely chopped
2 tablespoons lemon juice
200g/7 oz dried apricots
2 tablespoons seedless raisins
60g/2 oz almonds, blanched and toasted

1 In a large saucepan heat oil or butter and fry the onion until pale golden in color. Add the rice and stir 30 seconds to coat with oil.

2 Add the hot water, salt, pepper, parsley and lemon juice. Cover and simmer for 10 minutes.

3 Stir in the apricots (whole), raisins and almonds and simmer for 5 minutes more. Remove from heat and allow to stand, covered, for 5 minutes before serving.

Serves 4 • Preparation 20 minutes • Cooking 30 minutes

Tortellini with Tomato Cream Sauce

60g/2 oz unsalted butter
1 small onion, very finely chopped
1 stalk celery, very finely chopped
400mL/14 oz tomato sauce
½ teaspoon sugar
150mL/5 oz crème fraîche
salt and freshly ground black pepper
600g/20 oz fresh or frozen tortellini (such as spinach and ricotta)
freshly grated Parmesan to serve

1 Heat the butter in a heavy based saucepan, then add the onion and celery and
   saute for 5 minutes, or until softened. Add the tomato sauce and sugar and
   bring to a boil. Reduce the heat and simmer, uncovered, for 30 minutes or until
   the sauce thickened.

2 Spoon in the crème fraîche, season and bring back to a boil, stirring. Simmer for
   1 minute, then add more salt and pepper if necessary.

3 Bring a large saucepan of salted water to a boil, add the pasta and cook for
   5–6 minutes, or until just firm in the center (al dente), then drain. Transfer to a
   warmed serving bowl and pour over the sauce. Serve with Parmesan.

Serves 4 • Preparation 25 minutes • Cooking 45 minutes

Fusilli with Eggplant and Tomatoes

2 medium eggplants
½ cup olive oil
1 clove garlic
4 medium tomatoes
salt and pepper
1–2 tablespoons basil, chopped
300g/10 oz dried corkscrew pasta (fusilli or rotini)
2 tablespoons grated Parmesan

1 Peel eggplant and cut into small dice. Pour half the olive oil into a frying pan and add garlic and diced eggplant. Sauté gently until tender.

2 Meanwhile, skin the tomatoes, remove seeds and dice the flesh.

3 Pour the remaining oil into the frying pan and add the diced tomatoes. Cook for about 5 minutes and add salt, pepper and basil.

4 Bring a large saucepan of salted water to a boil, add the pasta and cook for 8 minutes, or until just firm in the center (al dente) and drain. Toss in the eggplant and tomatoes and sprinkle with grated cheese and black pepper, mixing well.

Serves 4–6 • Preparation 20 minutes • Cooking 25 minutes

Potato Gnocchi

1kg/2 lb russet or Idaho potatoes
1¾ cups all-purpose flour

1 Scrub the potatoes and place in a pan with just enough water to cover them. Cover and boil the potatoes until tender without letting them break up. Drain and peel as soon as you can handle them. Push through a ricer or mash with potato masher until all chunks are broken down.

2 As soon as the purée is cool enough to handle, start beating in the flour, then as the dough stiffens, turn it out to knead on a floured board. Knead until you have a soft and elastic dough.

3 Next, take a handful of the dough and knead lightly, using flour to dust your hands and the work surface. Roll dough into a sausage shape. Cut into 1in/25mm slices.

4 Take a large, slim-pronged fork with round edges. Hold it in your left hand with the prongs down. Take a slice of dough and gently press the dough against the prongs with your thumb, letting the gnocchi roll off on to a clean cloth. Repeat with remaining dough. The gnocchi should curl up into crescent-shaped, ribbed shells as they roll off the fork. The indentation in the middle helps the gnocchi cook evenly and the grooves hold the sauce.

5 Drop the gnocchi (about 20 at a time) into a large pan of boiling salted water. When they are ready they will float to the surface. Cook them another 10 seconds, then remove with a slotted spoon to a warm dish. Sprinkle them with freshly grated Parmesan and pieces of butter and toss lightly. Serve immediately.

Serves 4 • Preparation 1 hour • Cooking 40 minutes

Pasta with Double Tomato Sauce

1 tablespoon extra virgin olive oil
1 red onion, finely chopped
2 stalks celery, finely chopped
400g/14 oz canned chopped tomatoes
1 tablespoon tomato paste
1 cup vegetable stock
250g/8 oz cherry tomatoes, halved
1 teaspoon brown sugar
sea salt and freshly ground black pepper
340g/12 oz dried pasta, such as penne or mostaccioli
⅓ cup crème fraîche (optional)

1 Heat the oil in a large, heavy-based saucepan, then add the red onion and celery and
   cook uncovered for 5 minutes over a medium heat, until the vegetables are tender.
   Add the chopped tomatoes, tomato paste and stock and bring to a boil. Simmer,
   uncovered, for 15 minutes, stirring occasionally, until reduced and thickened.

2 Add the cherry tomatoes and the sugar and season generously, then stir gently for
   about 3 minutes, until heated through.

3 Bring a large saucepan of salted water to a boil, add the pasta and cook for 8 minutes
   or until just firm in the center (al dente) and drain. Pour the sauce over the pasta, toss
   gently to avoid breaking the cherry tomatoes and serve with a dollop of crème fraîche,
   if desired.

Serves 4 • Preparation 30 minutes • Cooking 45 minutes

Pasta Primavera

60g/2 oz butter
250g/8 oz baby spinach
500g/1 lb fresh peas, shelled
500g/1 lb fava beans, shelled
salt and freshly ground black pepper
⅓ cup crème fraîche
1 bunch green onions, finely sliced
2 tablespoons fresh parsley, finely chopped
75g/2½ oz Parmesan, grated
350g/12 oz dried pasta such as penne or mostaccioli

1 Melt the butter in a saucepan, add the spinach, cover, and cook for 5 minutes or until the leaves wilt. Set aside to cool. Cook the peas and beans in a little boiling salted water for 5 minutes, or until tender, then drain.

2 Blend the spinach and crème fraîche to a purée in a food processor or with a hand blender. Return the purée to the pan and stir in the peas and beans. Mix in the green onions and parsley, season and add half the Parmesan. Keep warm over a low heat.

3 Bring a large saucepan of salted water to a boil, add the pasta and cook for 8 minutes or until just firm in the center (al dente). Drain, then toss with the spinach mixture. Serve with the remaining Parmesan.

Serves 4 • Preparation 20 minutes • Cooking 25 minutes

Linguine with Leeks and Mushrooms

500g/1 lb leeks, sliced
250g/8 oz button mushrooms, sliced
1 bay leaf
40g/1½ oz butter
40g/1½ oz all-purpose flour
2 cups milk
2 tablespoons snipped fresh chives, plus extra to garnish
freshly ground black pepper
500g/1 lb fresh linguine

1 Steam the leeks and mushrooms with the bay leaf over a saucepan of boiling water for 10–15 minutes, until tender. Discard the bay leaf and keep the vegetables warm.

2 Melt the butter in a pan, add the flour and cook gently for 1 minute, stirring. Remove from the heat and gradually add the milk. Return to the heat and stir, until thickened. Reduce the heat and simmer for 2 minutes, stirring. Add the vegetables, chives and black pepper and heat through.

3 Bring a large saucepan of salted water to a boil, add the pasta and cook for 5–8 minutes or until just firm in the center (al dente). Drain and return to the pan, then add the leek and mushroom sauce and toss lightly to mix. Garnish with fresh chives.

Serves 4 • Preparation 30 minutes • Cooking 35 minutes

Tagliatelle Verde

75g/2½ oz green beans, halved crosswise
75g/2½ oz frozen chopped spinach, defrosted
150g/50 spinach tagliatelle or fettucine
2 teaspoons olive oil
30g/1 oz butter
1 clove garlic, crushed
3 tablespoons crème fraîche
½ teaspoon pesto
2 tablespoons freshly grated Parmesan, plus extra to sprinkle
freshly ground black pepper
2 teaspoons milk
1 tablespoon fresh parsley, chopped

1 Boil the green beans in a little water for 5–6 minutes, until cooked but still crunchy. Drain. Squeeze out any excess water from the spinach. Bring a large saucepan of salted water to a boil, add the tagliatelle and cook for 8 minutes or until just firm in the center (al dente). Drain, set aside and keep warm.

2 Meanwhile, heat the oil and butter in a saucepan, add the garlic and cook for 1 minute to soften. Stir in the crème fraîche, pesto, spinach and Parmesan and heat through. Add the beans and heat for an additional 1 minute, then season.

3 Add the pasta to the pan, then stir in the milk and most of the parsley. Toss well and heat through. Pile into bowls, sprinkle with Parmesan and garnish with the remaining parsley.

Serves 2 • Preparation 25 minutes • Cooking 20 minutes

Pasta with Butternut Squash and Sage Butter

2 tablespoons olive oil
2 cloves garlic, chopped
2 tablespoons fresh sage, chopped plus extra sprigs
1 butternut squash, peeled, seeded and cut into 1cm dice
350g/12 oz dried penne pasta
salt and freshly ground black pepper
75g/2½ oz butter
30g/1 oz Parmesan, grated
30g/1 oz pine nuts

1 Preheat the oven to 450°F/230°C. On a large rimmed baking sheet, toss the butternut squash with the oil, garlic, and 1 tablespoon of the chopped sage. Roast on the top rack of the oven for 20 minutes until browned and tender, turning once halfway through the cooking.

2 Meanwhile, bring a large saucepan of salted water to a boil, add the pasta and cook for 8 minutes or until just firm in the center (al dente). Drain, reserving ⅓ cup of the cooking liquid, set aside and keep warm.

3 Melt the butter in a large frying pan, add the remaining chopped sage and fry gently for 2–3 minutes. Meanwhile, heat another frying pan and dry-fry the pine nuts for 3–4 minutes over a high heat, until golden.

4 Add the reserved cooking liquid to the butter, then add the pasta and cooked squash. Toss, then serve sprinkled with the Parmesan, pine nuts and black pepper. Garnish with extra sage.

Serves 4 • Preparation 30 minutes • Cooking 40 minutes

Shells with Tomato Eggplant and Feta

3 tablespoons olive oil
1 onion, finely chopped
1 eggplant, diced
400g/14 oz can tomato sauce
300g/10 oz dried stortini pasta
4 tablespoons crème fraîche
100g/3½ oz feta, crumbled
¼ bunch fresh oregano or basil, chopped

1 Heat 1 tablespoon of the oil in a large heavy-based frying pan. Sauté the
   onion over a low heat for 5 minutes or until softened but not browned, stirring
   occasionally. Add the remaining oil and stir in the eggplant. Cook over a
   medium heat, stirring, for 10 minutes or until the eggplant is soft and golden
   brown. Add the tomato sauce and season with salt and pepper. Cover and
   simmer for 5 minutes or until slightly thickened.

2 Bring a large saucepan of salted water to a boil, add the pasta and cook for
   8 minutes or until just firm in the center (al dente). Drain well. Stir the crème
   fraîche into the sauce, then add the pasta and toss gently. Top with feta,
   oregano and basil.

Serves 4 • Preparation 30 minutes • Cooking 35 minutes

Penne with Peppers and Mascarpone

2 tablespoons olive oil
1 clove garlic, crushed
2 red onions, chopped
1 red, 1 yellow and 1 green bell pepper, cut into ½ in/15mm pieces
275g/9 oz dried penne pasta
200g/7 oz mascarpone cheese
juice of ½ lemon
½ bunch fresh flat-leaf parsley, chopped
freshly ground black pepper
⅓ cup freshly grated Parmesan

1 Heat the oil in a large frying pan and fry the garlic, onions and pepper for 10 minutes, stirring frequently, or until the vegetables have softened. Bring a large saucepan of salted water to a boil, add the pasta and cook for 8 minutes or until just firm in the center (al dente). Drain, set aside and keep warm.

2 Stir half the mascarpone, the lemon juice, parsley and seasoning into the pepper mixture. Cook for 5 minutes or until the mascarpone melts.

3 Stir the remaining mascarpone into the pasta, then add to the pepper mixture, tossing together well. Serve with a sprinkling of Parmesan.

Serves 4 • Preparation 25 minutes • Cooking 30 minutes

Pasta with Spring Vegetables

500g/1 lb dried pasta, such as shells or corkscrews
salt and freshly ground black pepper
300g/10 oz broccoli, cut into small florets
300g/10 oz fresh asparagus, trimmed and cut in half
60g/2 oz butter
2 cloves garlic, crushed
400g/14 oz fresh button mushrooms, sliced thickly
1 cup frozen peas
1 cup heavy cream
handful fresh basil leaves, coarsely chopped
freshly grated Parmesan cheese

1 Bring a large pot of salted water to a boil. Add pasta and cook for 8 minutes, or until just firm in the center (al dente.) Remove pasta with slotted spoon to reserve boiling water for the vegetables.

2 Add the broccoli to boiling water for about 4 minutes, remove and refresh under cold water. Set aside. Add asparagus to boiling water and cook for 3 minutes. Drain, refresh under cold water and set aside.

3 Melt half the butter on low heat in a large skillet. Add garlic and cook for a few minutes. Turn the heat up to medium high and add mushrooms, broccoli, asparagus and peas. Season with salt and pepper. Add cream and cook until sauce has reduced and thickened. Add remaining butter to the pan, plus the pasta and toss to coat. Add basil and freshly grated Parmesan cheese and stir until combined. Serve with extra cheese.

Serves 4 • Preparation 30 minutes • Cooking 30 minutes

Gnocchi Al Forno

400g/14 oz fresh gnocchi (see recipe on page 111)
1 tablespoon pine nuts
125g/4 oz mascarpone cheese
125g/4 oz blue cheese such as Gorgonzola
salt and freshly ground black pepper

1 Bring a large saucepan of salted water to a boil, add the gnocchi and cook until it begins to float. Drain well, then transfer to a shallow ovenproof dish.

2 Arrange oven rack so it is at least 6 in/15cm from the heat source. Preheat broiler. Toast pine nuts in dry skillet over medium heat for 2–3 minutes, or until golden, stirring, as they can burn quickly.

3 In a saucepan, warm mascarpone and blue cheese over low heat until melted. Season with salt and pepper. Spoon over gnocchi and broil for 2–3 minutes, until bubbling and golden. Top with pine nuts.

Serves 4 • Preparation 20 minutes • Cooking 20 minutes

Cappellini with Tomatoes, Garlic and Basil

½ cup olive oil
6 cloves garlic, thinly sliced
550g/20 oz Roma or plum tomatoes, seeded and diced
½ bunch basil, finely chopped
salt and freshly ground black pepper
500g/1 lb dried cappellini or thin spaghetti

1 Heat half the oil in a pan, add the garlic, and cook over a medium heat, until the garlic is slightly browned and golden.
2 Reduce the heat, and add tomatoes, basil, salt and pepper, and cook for 5 minutes (or until tomatoes are just heated through). Bring a large saucepan of salted water to a boil, add the pasta and cook for 5–8 minutes or until just firm in the center (al dente). Add remaining oil to the cooked pasta.
3 Serve tomato mixture over pasta.

Serves 4–6 • Preparation 20 minutes • Cooking 25 minutes

Main Courses

We've pulled together our favorite stir-fries, tarts and casseroles just bursting with fresh vegetables. Some familiar and some new versions of old favorites. Since vegetables are the star of show in these dishes, try to use vegetables that are in season and fresh at the market for the best results.

Tomato and Brie Tart

175g/6 oz all-purpose flour
sea salt
freshly ground black pepper
75g/2½ oz butter, diced
½ cup milk
2 medium egg yolks
1 clove garlic, crushed
1 tablespoon whole grain mustard
60g/2 oz Cheddar, grated
4 ripe tomatoes, sliced
125g/4 oz brie, thinly sliced

Herb oil
¼ bunch fresh basil, finely shredded
¼ bunch fresh parsley, finely chopped
2 tablespoons extra virgin olive oil

1 Sift the flour and a pinch of sea salt into a bowl, then rub the butter in using your fingertips, until it resembles fine breadcrumbs. Add 2 tablespoons of cold water and mix to a dough. Cover and refrigerate for 20 minutes. Roll out on floured surface and transfer to an 8 in/20cm tart pan. Refrigerate for an additional 10 minutes.

2 Preheat oven to 375°F/190°C. Blind bake the tart crust by lining with parchment paper and dried beans or pie weights for 10–12 minutes or until crust is slightly golden. Carefully remove weights and paper, and bake for an additional 5 minutes. Let cool. Reduce oven temperature to 350°F/180°C.

3 In a bowl, combine milk, egg yolks, and garlic. Season with salt and pepper. Spread mustard in a thin layer on the bottom of the tart crust. Top with grated Cheddar, sliced tomatoes, and brie. Pour egg mixture over the top and cook for 30–35 minutes, until eggs are set and golden. Combine herbs and olive oil and drizzle over the tart before serving.

Serves 4 • Preparation 1 hour • Cooking 1 hour 20 minutes

Stir Fried Vegetables

2 tablespoons vegetable oil
2 in/5cm piece fresh ginger, peeled, finely chopped
3 cloves garlic, finely chopped
2 tablespoons dry sherry
1 yellow bell pepper, seeded and chopped into 1 in/25mm pieces
1 red bell pepper, seeded and chopped into 1 in/25mm pieces
2 medium carrots, peeled and thinly sliced on the diagonal
350g/12 oz broccoli, cut into 1 in/25mm florets and stalks thinly sliced
300g/10 oz button or cremini mushrooms, thickly sliced
2 tablespoons soy sauce
8 green onions, cut into 1cm diagonal slices

1 Heat a large wok or heavy-based frying pan over a high heat for 1 minute. Add the oil and rotate the wok or pan to coat the base and lower sides.
2 Add the ginger and garlic and fry, stirring, for 30 seconds. Add the sherry and cook for a further 15 seconds. Add the pepper and carrots and continue to stir – fry for 5 minutes or until the vegetables start to soften.
3 Add the broccoli, mushrooms and soy sauce and fry, stirring, for 3 minutes or until all the vegetables are just tender. Add the green onions and stir-fry for 1 minute. Serve with rice or noodles.

Serves 4 • Preparation 30 minutes • Cooking 20 minutes

Stuffed Eggplant

2 tablespoons olive oil
2 eggplants
50g/15 oz tomatoes, chopped
2 teaspoons dried oregano
3 cloves garlic, chopped
salt and freshly ground black pepper
2 tablespoons tomato paste
125g/4 oz Gruyère cheese, thinly sliced

1 Preheat the oven to 400°F/200°C. Lightly oil a baking sheet. Slice the eggplant down the middle lengthwise. Carefully scoop out the flesh of the eggplant, leaving at least ¼ in/6mm of flesh still on the skin. Chop the flesh into small pieces.

2 In a large skillet, heat oil, and add chopped eggplant, tomatoes, oregano, and garlic. Season with salt and pepper. Cook until slightly softened, about 5 minutes, stirring occasionally. Add tomato paste and cook for another 5 minutes.

3 Meanwhile, place the eggplant halves on the baking sheet, brush the insides with oil and cook for 10–12 minutes, until almost tender. Fill the eggplant with the tomato mixture, cover with the Gruyère and return to the oven. Cook for 10 minutes, or until the cheese has browned.

Serves 4 • Preparation 35 minutes • Cooking 40 minutes

Couscous with Roasted Vegetables

4 parsnips, cut into chunks
2 sweet potatoes, cut into chunks
4 turnips, quartered
2 cloves garlic, crushed
5 tablespoons olive oil
4 tablespoons apple or red currant jelly
300g/10 oz couscous
500g/1 lb tomatoes, chopped
handful each of fresh parsley, chives and basil, chopped
juice of 1 lemon
300g/10 oz broccoli, cut into florets

1 Preheat the oven to 400°F/200°C. Cook the parsnips in a saucepan of boiling salted water for 2 minutes, then drain. Place on rimmed baking sheet with sweet potatoes, turnips, garlic and 3 tablespoons of the oil, turning to coat. Sprinkle with salt and pepper and roast for 30 minutes, or until lightly browned. Remove from oven.

2 In a sauce pan, melt the jelly with 80mL or 5 tablespoons of water for 2–3 minutes until syrupy. Gently turn the roasted vegetables and cover with syrup. Add broccoli to pan and return to the oven for 10 more minutes.

3 Prepare the couscous according to the instructions on the package. Heat the rest of the oil in a frying pan and cook the tomatoes for 2–3 minutes, until softened. Stir in the couscous, herbs, and lemon juice. Top with roasted vegetables and serve.

Serves 4 • Preparation 40 minutes • Cooking 1 hour

Harvest Vegetable Bake

1 onion, sliced
2 leeks, sliced
2 stalks celery, chopped
2 carrots, thinly sliced
1 red pepper, seeded and sliced
500g/1 lb mixed root vegetables, such as sweet potato, parsnip and turnip, cubed
175g/6 oz mushrooms, sliced
400g/14 oz canned diced tomatoes
½ cup white wine
1 teaspoon dried thyme
1 teaspoon dried oregano
freshly ground black pepper
fresh basil, to garnish

1 Preheat the oven to 360°F/180°C. Place the onion, leeks, celery, carrots, pepper, cubed root vegetables and mushrooms in a large ovenproof casserole dish and mix well. Stir in the tomatoes, cider, thyme, oregano and black pepper.

2 Cover and bake in the center of the oven for 1–1½ hours, until the vegetables are cooked through and tender, stirring once or twice. Garnish with fresh herbs.

Serves 4 • Preparation 30 minutes • Cooking 1 hour 30 minutes

Zucchini and Cheese Gratin

4 large zucchini, sliced diagonally
400g/14 oz/ canned diced tomatoes, drained
2 tablespoons fresh basil, shredded
sea salt and freshly ground black pepper
250g/8 oz fresh mozzarella, drained and sliced
60g/2 oz freshly grated Parmesan
1 tablespoon extra virgin olive oil

1 Preheat the oven to 400°F/200°C. Blanch the zucchini in boiling salted water for
   about 4 minutes, drain well and then thoroughly dry using paper towel.
2 Layer half the zucchini in a shallow, ovenproof baking dish, spread with half of the
   tomatoes, half the basil, half the mozzarella, salt and pepper.
3 Repeat layering the zucchini, tomatoes, basil, mozzarella and top with Parmesan.
   Drizzle with olive oil and bake for 25 minutes, or until golden and bubbling.

Serves 4 • Preparation 25 minutes • Cooking 35 minutes

Sesame Stir Fry

2 tablespoons sesame seeds
2 tablespoons peanut oil
1 clove garlic, roughly chopped
1 in/25mm piece fresh ginger, finely chopped
150g/50 oz broccoli, cut into very small florets
2 zucchini, halved lengthwise and finely sliced
170g/6 oz snowpeas
1 tablespoon rice wine or white wine
1 tablespoon soy sauce

1 Heat a wok. Add the sesame seeds and dry-fry for 2 minutes or until golden, shaking the pan frequently. Remove and set aside.

2 Add the oil to the wok, heat for 1 minute, then add the garlic and ginger and stir-fry over a medium heat for 1–2 minutes, until softened. Add the broccoli and stir-fry for an additional 2–3 minutes.

3 Add the zucchini and snowpeas and stir-fry for 3 minutes. Add the wine and stir, to loosen up the browned bits on the bottom of the pan. Add soy sauce and stir fry for 2 more minutes. Sprinke with sesame seeds and serve immediately.

Serves 4 • Preparation 20 minutes • Cooking 20 minutes

Vegetable Cheese Gratin

1 large butternut squash, peeled, seeded and cut into chunks
salt and freshly ground black pepper
3 tablespoons olive oil
1 large cauliflower, cut into florets
350g/12 oz mushrooms, sliced
2 tablespoons fresh white breadcrumbs
2 tablespoons freshly grated Parmesan

Sauce
60g/2 oz butter
60g/2 oz all-purpose flour
pinch of cayenne pepper
300mL/10 oz milk
1 teaspoon ground mustard powder
100g/3½ oz Cheddar cheese, grated

1 Preheat the oven to 400°F/200°C. Put the squash into an ovenproof dish, season, then
   drizzle over half the oil. Roast for 25 minutes, stirring once, until tender. Meanwhile,
   cook the cauliflower in boiling salted water for 5 minutes or until just tender. Drain,
   reserving 200mL/7oz of the cooking water, then refresh in cold water and set aside.
   Fry the mushrooms in the remaining oil for 4–5 minutes.

2 To make the sauce, melt the butter in a saucepan and stir in the flour and cayenne
   pepper. Cook for 2 minutes, then gradually stir in the reserved cooking liquid. Cook
   for 2–3 minutes, until thick, then gradually stir in the milk. Simmer, stirring, for
   10 minutes. Remove from the heat, then stir in the mustard and the cheese, until
   melted. Season to taste.

3 Reduce the oven temperature to 360°F/180°C. Add the cauliflower to the squash,
   then divide between four lightly buttered individual ovenproof dishes. Scatter over
   the mushrooms and pour over the sauce. Mix the breadcrumbs and Parmesan, then
   sprinkle over each dish. Bake for 30–35 minutes.

Serves 4 • Preparation 30 minutes • Cooking 1 hour 30 minutes

Pizza with Tomato, Zucchini and Red Onion

Pizza base
225g/8 oz whole wheat flour
2 teaspoons baking powder
60g/2 oz butter
100mL/3½ oz milk

Topping
1 tablespoon olive oil
2 small red onions, sliced
1 yellow bell pepper, sliced
2 small zucchini, sliced
1 clove garlic, crushed
5 tablespoons tomato paste
2 teaspoons dried mixed herbs
freshly ground black pepper
3 small Roma or plum tomatoes, sliced
100g/3½ oz Cheddar or Provolone cheese, grated
fresh basil to garnish (optional)

1 To make the pizza crust, place the flour and baking powder in a bowl, then rub in the butter. Stir in the milk to form a smooth dough and knead lightly.

2 Preheat the oven to 430°F/220°C. Heat the oil in a saucepan, then add the onions, pepper, zucchini and garlic and cook for 5 minutes or until softened, stirring occasionally. Set aside. Roll out the dough on a lightly floured surface to a circle about 25cm wide and place on a buttered baking sheet.

3 Mix together the tomato paste, mixed herbs and black pepper and spread over the dough. Top with the onion mixture.

4 Arrange the tomato slices on top and sprinkle with Cheddar. Bake for 25–30 minutes, until the cheese is golden brown and bubbling. Garnish with fresh basil if using.

Serves 4 • Preparation 40 minutes • Cooking 40 minutes

Classic Herb Omelet

2 large eggs
salt and freshly ground black pepper
15g/½ oz butter
2 tablespoons fresh mixed herbs, such as parsley and chives, chopped

1 Crack the eggs into a small bowl, then season. Mix lightly with a fork for about 20 seconds, until just blended.

2 Place a small non-stick frying pan over a high heat. When the pan is hot, add the butter and tilt the pan until it covers the base.

3 Pour the eggs into the pan, then tilt the pan so that the eggs cover the base and start to set. After about 10 seconds, use a spatula to pull the cooked egg gently from the edge of the pan towards the center, so that any uncooked egg runs underneath and sets. Continue pulling the edges until all the egg has set (this will take 2–3 minutes).

4 Sprinkle the herbs evenly over the omelet. Using the spatula, gently fold the omelet in half. Tilt the pan and slide the omelet onto a plate.

Serves 1 • Preparation 5 minutes • Cooking 5 minutes

Spinach Blue Cheese Tart

1 pre-made pie crust
250g/8 oz fresh spinach, stems removed
freshly ground black pepper
¼ teaspoon ground nutmeg
125g/4 oz blue cheese, such as Roquefort or Gorgonzola
1 egg, beaten
1 cup heavy cream

1 Preheat the oven to 400°F/200°C. Roll out the pastry on a lightly floured surface and use it to line a 9 in/23cm tart pan. Prick the pastry base with a fork and bake for 10 minutes or until lightly golden.

2 Meanwhile, rinse the spinach and place in a saucepan with the water clinging to its leaves. Cook covered for 3–4 minutes, until wilted. Drain, leave to cool slightly, then squeeze out the excess water. Evenly arrange into the pastry base, season with pepper and nutmeg, then add the cheese. Mix together the egg and cream and pour over the top.

3 Bake for 30 minutes or until the filling has risen and is golden. Let rest for 10 minutes before slicing.

Serves 6 • Preparation 20 minutes • Cooking 50 minutes

Noodles with Peanut Sauce

250g/8 oz dried fettucine or rice noodles
2 tablespoons canola or peanut oil
1 clove garlic, sliced
2 carrots, thinly sliced diagonally
150g/5 oz green beans, halved
150g/5 oz broccoli florets
1 red bell pepper, seeded and cut into matchsticks
4 green onions, thinly sliced diagonally
chopped fresh cilantro, to garnish
lime wedges

Sauce
⅓ cup smooth peanut butter
1 tablespoon tomato paste
1 tablespoon balsamic vinegar
sea salt and freshly ground black pepper

1 Cook the noodles until tender but, still a bit firm in the middle, about 1–2 minutes less than the directed amount of time. Drain and set aside. Mix together peanut butter sauce, tomato paste, balsamic vinegar, salt and pepper with about 200mL/7 oz cold water. Set aside.

2 Heat the oil in a wok or large frying pan until very hot. Add the garlic, carrots and green beans and stir-fry for 2 minutes, until slightly browned. Add the broccoli and stir-fry for 2–3 minutes or until softened. Add the red pepper and green onions, and cook for an additional minute.

3 Add the sauce and drained noodles to the pan. Stir fry for 4–5 minutes, until everything is incorporated and hot. Top with cilantro and a squeeze of lime.

Serves 4 • Preparation 35 minutes • Cooking 30 minutes

Mushroom Leek Pies

60g/2 oz butter
2 carrots, cut into matchsticks
1 teaspoon paprika
4 leeks, thinly sliced
2 cloves garlic, thinly sliced
250g/8 oz cremini or button mushrooms, sliced
5 tablespoons heavy cream
1–2 teaspoons soy sauce
2 tablespoons fresh parsley, chopped
lemon juice to taste
salt and freshly ground black pepper
2 sheets puff pastry, thawed overnight in the refrigerator
1 small egg, beaten

1 Preheat the oven to 400°F/200°C. Melt the butter in a frying pan, add the carrots and paprika and fry gently for 5 minutes, or until softened. Stir in the leeks and garlic and fry for 2 minutes, then add the mushrooms and fry for 5 minutes, stirring frequently until the vegetables are tender and any liquid has evaporated.

2 Stir in the cream and soy sauce, then simmer for 2 minutes. Add the parsley and lemon juice and season. Cool to room temperature.

3 Gently roll out puff pastry on a floured surface. Cut out 2 circles on each sheet, using a plate or cutter as a guide. Divide filling among circles, and trace the outer edges of the crust with beaten egg. Fold the pastry over to enclose and seal, pinching with fingers or a fork. Brush the tops of each pie with remaining egg wash. Bake on the top rack of the oven for 25 minutes or until puffed and golden brown.

Serves 4 • Preparation 30 minutes • Cooking 40 minutes

Frittata with Corn, Zucchini and Red Pepper

2 tablespoons olive oil
1 onion, chopped
2 cloves garlic, crushed
3 zucchini, sliced
1 red and 1 yellow bell pepper, sliced
125g/½ cup fresh or canned corn
6 medium eggs
¼ bunch fresh parsley, chopped
¼ bunch fresh basil, chopped
1 teaspoon cayenne pepper
salt and freshly ground black pepper

1 Preheat the oven to 350°F/175°C. Heat the oil in a 10-inch, oven-safe nonstick skillet (without a rubber or plastic handle) over medium heat. Add the onion, garlic, zucchini and peppers. Saute until tender and golden, about 10 minutes. Stir in the corn.

2 Beat eggs til bubbly. Add parsley, basil, cayenne, salt and pepper. Pour mixture into the pan spread the vegetables evenly in the pan. Cook over low heat for 5–6 minutes, until the edges start to set. Transfer the skillet to the oven and bake until the frittata is slightly puffed and egg mixture has set, 25–30 minutes.

3 Cool for 5 minutes. Using a silicone or rubber spatula, loosen the edge of the frittata and slide onto a platter. Cut into wedges and serve.

Serves 4 • Preparation 25 minutes • Cooking 25 minutes

Vegetable Tacos

1 tablespoon canola oil
1 onion, chopped
1 green bell pepper, diced
2 cloves garlic, finely chopped
1 jalapeno pepper, finely chopped
2 teaspoons ground cumin
1 teaspoon hot chilli powder
400g/14 oz canned diced tomatoes
1 tablespoon tomato paste
3 carrots, cubed
175g/6 oz rutabaga, cubed
175g/6 oz mushrooms, chopped
3 stalks celery, finely chopped
½ cup vegetable stock
freshly ground black pepper
420g/15 oz canned red kidney beans, drained and rinsed
fresh cilantro to garnish

1 Preheat the oven to 360°F/180°C. Heat the oil in a large Dutch oven or stock pot. Add the onion, green pepper, garlic and jalapeno and cook for 5 minutes or until softened, stirring occasionally.

2 Add the cumin and chilli powder and cook, stirring gently for 1 minute to release the flavors. Mix in the tomatoes, tomato paste, carrots, rutabaga, mushrooms, celery, stock and black pepper.

3 Cover and cook in the oven for 45 minutes, stirring once. Add the kidney beans, cover again and cook for an additional 15–20 minutes or until all the vegetables are tender. Garnish with fresh cilantro.

Serves 4 • Preparation 35 minutes • Cooking 1 hour 20 minutes

Sides

Make your entrees even more tempting with these fabulous vegetable accompaniments. With the help of these inspirational recipes, you can transform your vegetables into delicious side dishes. From light favorites to decadent creamy comfort foods, these sides make the meal.

Roasted Peppers and Onions

4 onions, quartered
3 sprigs of thyme
100mL vegetable stock or white wine
3 tablespoons cider vinegar
2 tablespoons olive oil
1 tablespoon molasses or brown sugar
2 teaspoons caraway seeds
4 cloves garlic, peeled and left whole
salt and freshly ground black pepper
3 green bell peppers, cut into wide strips

1 Preheat the oven to 400°F/200°C. Place the onions, thyme, stock or wine, vinegar, oil, molasses or sugar, caraway seeds and garlic in an ovenproof dish. Season, cover with foil and bake for 30 minutes or until the onions have softened slightly.

2 Remove the foil, baste the onions with the cooking liquid, then re-cover and return to the oven for 30 minutes or until the onions are just tender. Add a little water if the liquid has evaporated.

3 Increase the oven heat to 480°F/250°C. Remove the foil from the dish and stir in the peppers. Return the dish to the oven, uncovered, and cook the vegetables for 8–10 minutes, turning halfway through cooking, until browned and caramelized.

Serves 6 • Preparation 20 minutes • Cooking 1 hour 10 minutes

Herbed Mashed Potatoes

salt and freshly ground black pepper
1kg/2 lb russet or Idaho potatoes, quartered
3 tablespoons olive oil
1 tablespoon fresh chives, chopped
30g/1 oz butter, melted

1 Place potatoes in a large saucepan. Cover with cold water, season with salt, and bring to a boil. Cook for 20 minutes, or until fork tender. Drain and peel (if desired). Mash with fork or potato masher, season with salt, pepper and olive oil.
2 Transfer potatoes to serving dish. Top with chives and melted butter.

Serves 6 • Preparation 10 minutes • Cooking 25 minutes

Green Beans with Walnut Dressing

450g/15 oz green beans
2 tablespoons walnut oil
1 tablespoon olive oil
1 tablespoon white wine vinegar
1 teaspoon Dijon mustard
freshly ground black pepper

1 Cook the beans in a saucepan of salted, boiling water for 5–6 minutes, until tender. Drain.
2 Mix walnut oil, olive oil, vinegar, mustard and pepper in a small bowl. Toss beans in dressing and serve hot or cold.

Serves 4–6 • Preparation 10 minutes • Cooking 6 minutes

Cheesy Cauliflower

salt and freshly ground black pepper
1 large cauliflower, cut into florets

Cheese sauce
60g/2 oz butter
60g/2 oz all-purpose flour
½ teaspoon dry mustard powder
pinch of cayenne pepper
100mL/20 oz milk
125g/4 oz aged Cheddar cheese, grated

1 Bring a large saucepan of water to a boil, then add half a teaspoon of salt. Add the cauliflower florets cover and cook for 7–10 minutes, until tender. Drain and set aside.

2 To make the sauce, melt the butter in a large heavy-based pan over a low heat. Add the flour, mustard powder and cayenne pepper and stir briskly to form a smooth thick paste. Cook for 2 minutes, stirring all the time.

3 Remove from the heat and add the milk little by little, stirring each time so there are no lumps. Return the pan to the heat, increase the heat to medium and simmer the sauce for 5–7 minutes, stirring constantly until thickened.

4 Preheat the oven to 440°F/220°C. Take the pan off the heat again and add 2½ oz/75g of the cheese, stirring until it melts into the sauce. Season with salt and black pepper. Put the cauliflower into an ovenproof dish, pour over the sauce, then sprinkle the remaining cheese on top. Bake for 10–15 minutes, until the top is golden.

Serves 4 • Preparation 25 minutes • Cooking 35 minutes

Caramelized Shallots

600g/20 oz shallots or pearl onions
2 tablespoons olive oil
1–2 tablespoons fresh rosemary, chopped
freshly ground black pepper

1 Preheat the oven to 400°F/200°C. Place the shallots in a roasting pan, drizzle over the oil, sprinkle with the rosemary and black pepper, then toss to mix.

2 Cook in the oven for 30–40 minutes, stirring once or twice. The shallots should be tender and golden brown. Serve hot.

Serves 4 • Preparation 15 minutes • Cooking 40 minutes

Sesame Spinach

750g/1½ lb fresh spinach, stems removed
1 tablespoon peanut oil
1 teaspoon sesame oil
3 cloves garlic, chopped
2 tablespoons sesame seeds
juice of ½ lemon and ¼ teaspoon finely grated lemon zest (optional)
salt and freshly ground black pepper

1 Place the spinach in a large bowl, cover with boiling water, then leave for
  2–3 minutes. Drain, then refresh under cold running water. Squeeze out any
  excess water, then coarsely chop.
2 Heat the peanut and sesame oil in a wok or large, heavy-based frying pan.
  Add the garlic and the sesame seeds and fry for 1–2 minutes, until the garlic
  has begun to brown and the seeds have started to pop.
3 Stir in the spinach and cook for 1–2 minutes, until heated through. Remove
  from the heat, rest for 2 minutes, add the lemon juice and zest (if using),
  season and mix well.

Serves 6 • Preparation 10 minutes • Cooking 10 minutes

Fingerling Potatoes with Lemon and Olives

1 lemon
750g/1½ lb fingerling or new potatoes, halved
2 cloves garlic, sliced
2 tablespoons olive oil
salt and freshly ground black pepper
15g/½ oz butter
60g/2 oz pitted green olives, quartered

1 Preheat the oven to 430°F/220°C. Squeeze the juice from 1 half and chop the other half into small pieces.
2 Toss the potatoes, lemon juice, chopped lemon, garlic and oil together. Season, then arrange in a single layer in a shallow roasting pan and dot with the butter. Cook for 25–30 minutes, shaking the tin occasionally, until the potatoes are tender and golden brown. Stir in the olives just before serving.

Serves 4 • Preparation 20 minutes • Cooking 30 minutes

Bok Choy with Oyster Sauce

400g/14oz bok choy
3 tablespoons oyster sauce (vegetarian if preferred))
1 tablespoon peanut oil
salt

1   Trim boy choy stalks, separate leaves and rinse thoroughly. In a small bowl, mix oysters sauce and oil. Reserve.
2   Boil bok choy in a large pot of salted water. Cook, uncovered for 3 minutes or until tender. Drain thoroughly and toss with dressing.

Serves 4 • Preparation 10 minutes • Cooking 5 minutes

Spicy Cauliflower with Garlic

2 slices wheat bread
1 cauliflower, cut into florets
salt and freshly ground black pepper
⅓ cup olive oil
1 clove garlic, crushed
½–1 teaspoon red pepper flakes
8 black olives, pitted and halved
1 tablespoon capers

1 Toast bread til crisp. Process in a food processor or grater to make fresh
   bread crumbs.
2 Place the cauliflower in a saucepan, cover with boiling water and add a
   little salt. Return to a boil, simmer for 1 minute or until slightly softened,
   then drain well.
3 Heat the oil in a large, heavy-based frying pan. Add the garlic, red pepper
   and cauliflower and cook for 3 minutes, or until the cauliflower starts to
   brown. Add the olives, capers, breadcrumbs and seasoning. Cook for an
   additional minute to incorporate the bread crumbs.

Serves 4 • Preparation 15 minutes • Cooking 30 minutes

Sweet Potato and Onion Gratin

3 tablespoons olive oil
3 onions, sliced into thin rings
750g/1½ lbs sweet potatoes, thinly sliced
salt and freshly ground black pepper
150mL vegetable stock

1 Heat half the oil in a wok or large, heavy-based frying pan. Add the onions and
   cook on medium low heat for 8–10 minutes, until golden brown.

2 Preheat the oven to 400°F/200°C. Arrange one-third of the sweet potatoes in a
   baking dish and top with half the onions. Season and cover with another layer of
   sweet potato. Cover with the remaining onions, season, then finish with a final
   layer of sweet potatoes.

3 Pour the stock over the potato mixture, cover with foil, and bake for 40–45 minutes,
   or until the potatoes are just tender. Remove the foil and drizzle with the remaining
   oil. Increase the oven temperature to 450°F/230°C and bake for an additional
   8–10 minutes, until browned.

Serves 6 • Preparation 20 minutes • Cooking 1 hour

Asian Stir Fry

½ cucumber
2 tablespoons sesame seeds
1 tablespoon canola oil
4 carrots, cut into matchsticks
250g/8 oz snowpeas
6 green onions, chopped
juice of ½ a lemon
freshly ground black pepper

1 Peel the cucumber, cut it in half lengthwise and scoop out the seeds. Slice into half moons.

2 Heat a non-stick wok or large frying pan. Add the sesame seeds and dry-fry for 1 minute tossing constantly until toasted. Remove and set aside. Add the oil, then the cucumber and carrots and stir-fry over a high heat for 2 minutes. Add the snowpeas and green onions and stir-fry for a further 2–3 minutes, until all the vegetables are cooked but still crisp.

3 Add lemon juice, sesame seeds, and black pepper. Stir fry for a another minute to heat through.

Serves 4 • Preparation 10 minutes • Cooking 6 minutes

Baked Polenta

1 tablespoon olive oil
1 small onion, finely chopped
2 cloves garlic, crushed
½ teaspoon ground cilantro
750g/3½ lb fresh spinach
1 cup heavy cream
60g/2 oz Gorgonzola or blue cheese, crumbled
pinch of ground nutmeg
salt and freshly ground black pepper
1 lb ready-made polenta, thinly sliced
150g/5 oz fresh mozzarella cheese, thinly sliced

1 Preheat the oven to 450°F/230°C. Heat the oil in a saucepan and gently fry the onion, garlic and cilantro for 5 minutes, or until the onion is softened.

2 Blanch the spinach in boiling salted water for 1 minute, refresh under cold running water, then drain well and squeeze out any excess moisture. Stir the spinach into the pan with the cream, Gorgonzola, nutmeg, salt and pepper. Bring to a simmer, then transfer to a large, shallow, ovenproof dish.

3 Arrange the polenta and mozzarella slices over the top of the spinach mixture, pressing down well. Bake for 15 minutes or until bubbling. Turn on the broiler and broil for 1–2 minutes, until slightly browned.

Serves 4 • Preparation 30 minutes • Cooking 30 minutes

Index